★ CAREERS IN THE US MILITARY

SERVICE PROVIDERS

J. P. Miller

Rourke
Educational Media

A Division of
Carson Dellosa Education

ROURKE'S SCHOOL to HOME CONNECTIONS
BEFORE AND DURING READING ACTIVITIES

Before Reading: *Building Background Knowledge and Vocabulary*

Building background knowledge can help children process new information and build upon what they already know. Before reading a book, it is important to tap into what children already know about the topic. This will help them develop their vocabulary and increase their reading comprehension.

Questions and Activities to Build Background Knowledge:
1. Look at the front cover of the book and read the title. What do you think this book will be about?
2. What do you already know about this topic?
3. Take a book walk and skim the pages. Look at the table of contents, photographs, captions, and bold words. Did these text features give you any information or predictions about what you will read in this book?

Vocabulary: *Vocabulary Is Key to Reading Comprehension*
Use the following directions to prompt a conversation about each word.
- Read the vocabulary words.
- What comes to mind when you see each word?
- What do you think each word means?

Vocabulary Words:
- civilian
- dignity
- esprit de corp
- intramural
- military base
- morale

During Reading: *Reading for Meaning and Understanding*

To achieve deep comprehension of a book, children are encouraged to use close reading strategies. During reading, it is important to have children stop and make connections. These connections result in deeper analysis and understanding of a book.

Close Reading a Text
During reading, have children stop and talk about the following:
- Any confusing parts
- Any unknown words
- Text-to-text, text-to-self, text-to-world connections
- The main idea in each chapter or heading

Encourage children to use context clues to determine the meaning of any unknown words. These strategies will help children learn to analyze the text more thoroughly as they read.

When you are finished reading this book, turn to the next-to-last page for **After-Reading Questions** and an **Activity**.

TABLE OF CONTENTS

The Importance of Services 4
Work and Play 8
Having What It Takes 28
Memory Game 30
Index 31
After-Reading Questions 31
Activity 31
About the Author 32

THE IMPORTANCE OF SERVICES

The heart of any **military base** is its services unit. It is the first stop for new military members. The Service Providers who work there can affect the way others see the base.

Service Providers have the job of making military members happy. The things they do are very similar to neighborhood Parks and Recreation Departments. Even during combat, Service Providers are there to feed and plan fun activities for military members.

military base (MIL-i-ter-ee base): the headquarters or main place for part of the military

The US Military has five branches: the Army, Air Force, Navy, Marines, and Coast Guard. Each branch has many careers, and they all work together. The meals prepared by Service Providers give other military members the strength needed to do their jobs. Service Providers help keep military members fit for duty. Recreation activities allow military members and their families to reenergize and have fun together.

Service Providers work early mornings, late nights, weekends, and holidays. Their work is important for the happiness of everyone on a base. It is their job to maintain high **morale**.

morale (muh-RAL): the mood or spirit of a person or group

WORK AND PLAY

Service Providers help make time away from work fun. Fitness Specialists plan team games and practice times. They make sure that sports equipment and playing fields are clean and safe.

Fitness Specialists organize **intramural** team sports on military bases. Teams play against each other in basketball, flag football, softball, and volleyball. All of them want to be the champions!

intramural (IN-truh-myur-uhl): contained in a group, community, or institution, such as branch of the military

Fitness Specialists help others stay fit. They can offer advice on the best ways to exercise.

To do well as a Fitness Specialist, it is important to be a good leader. You should also know about sports and fitness and be active yourself.

A FIT MILITARY

Fitness is very important to the military. Members must be in good physical shape to go on missions. Most military bases have more than one fitness center.

Before the sun comes up, the smell of food fills the air. The Food Service Specialists are already hard at work cooking for huge groups of people.

They stand over giant pots cooking from their recipes. Each dish is made from scratch, just like food that the other military members might have at home. Food Service Specialists make sure that meals are nutritious and taste good.

FOOD SERVICE EVERYWHERE

Food Service Specialists are on every military base, ship, and submarine. Where the military go, Food Service Specialists go. They even take mobile kitchens to the battlefield. In one day, they serve over a million meals worldwide.

Food Service Specialists plan menus for everyone on the base. They order food and supplies and cook the food. They keep the kitchen organized and clean.

To do well as a Food Service Specialist, it is important to follow directions. Having a good attitude can lift morale. Food Service Specialists must enjoy serving others...and cooking, of course!

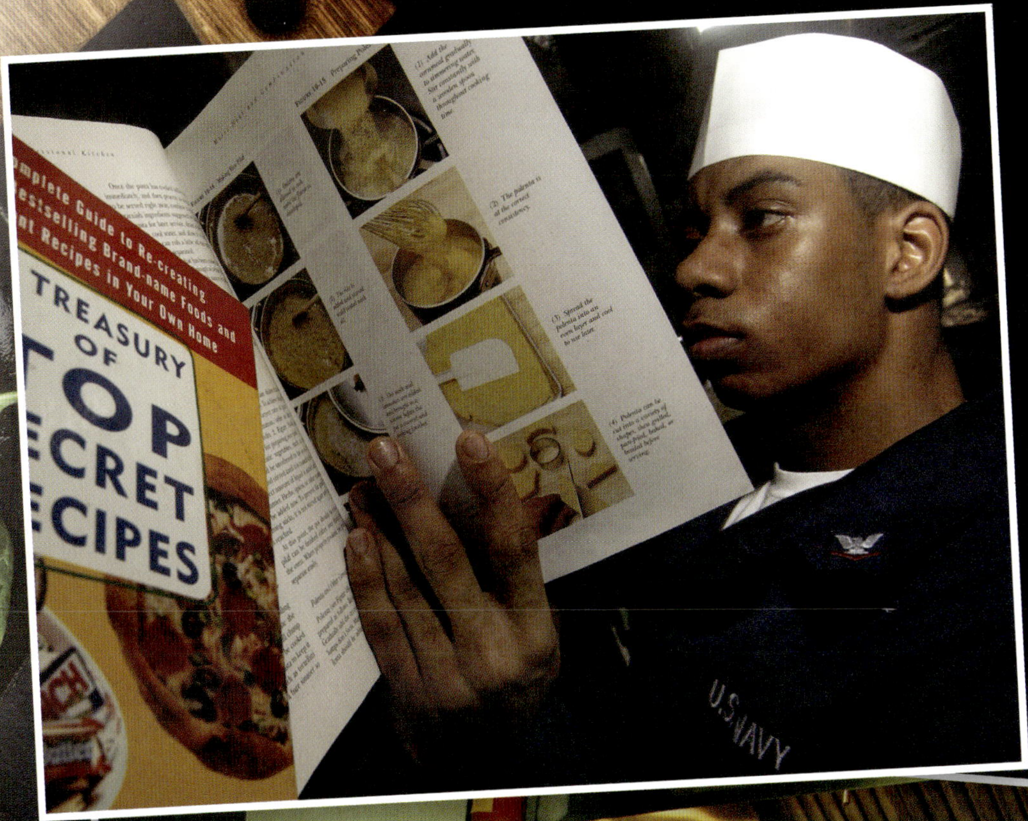
TREASURY
OF
U.S. NAVY
Proper Cooking Temperatures

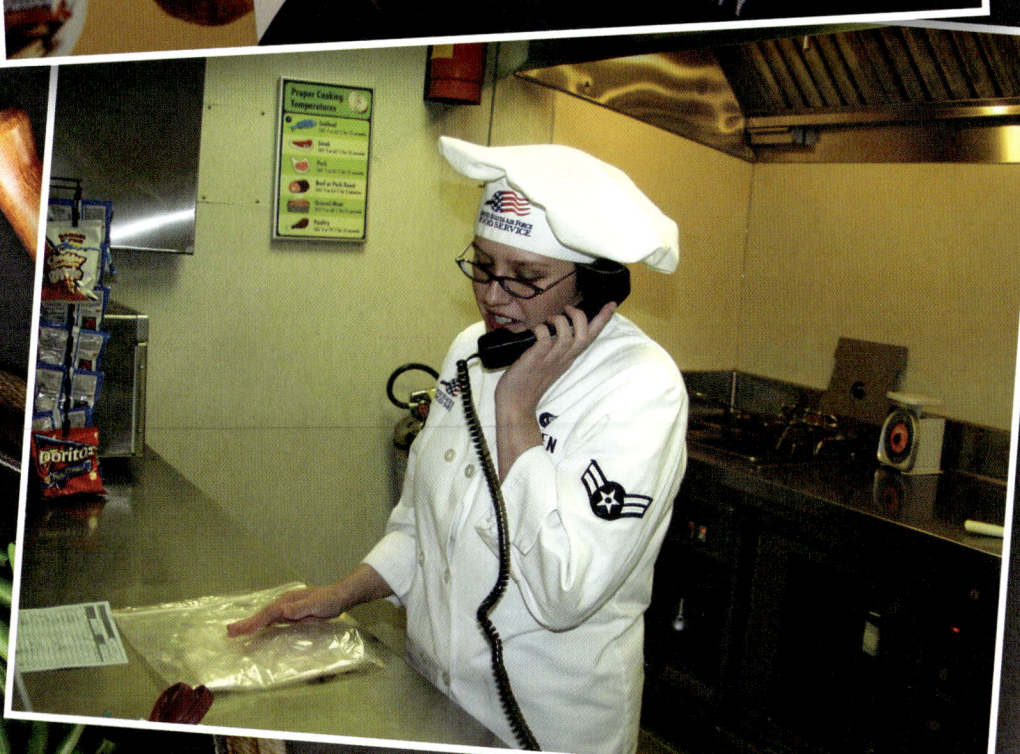

Travel can be tiring. After a long trip, military members often want to relax. Lodging Specialists give them a place to do this. These Specialists organize housing for military members and their families.

Base lodging is like a hotel except that it is located on a military base. Lodging Specialists are like Guest Services workers at a hotel. They greet guests with a smile and make them feel welcome.

HOME AWAY FROM HOME

Lodging Specialists want guests to feel at home when they are away from home. Some rooms even have cold drinks, candy, and snacks in them to help guests relax.

Lodging Specialists must be friendly and ready to answer questions about the base and local areas. They also take reservations for air crews, inspection teams, and other large groups.

To do well as a Lodging Specialist, it is important to have great customer service skills. A visit to base lodging can change how a visitor feels about a military base. A Lodging Specialist must make that visit a good one!

Mortuary Affairs Specialists have difficult jobs. They take care of things when a military member dies in service.

These experts work with a military officer to transport the military member's body back home safely. Mortuary Affairs Specialists prepare the body for burial and dress them in their final uniform.

A PLACE OF LOVE
Preparing the final uniform is done out of appreciation and respect. Mortuary Affairs Specialists pick out a brand new uniform. They press it and stay until any new badges, name tags, and ribbons are measured and properly placed.

The death of a military member is a somber time. Mortuary Affairs Specialists do all they can to make this difficult time easier for people who knew the military member who has died. They do it with **dignity**, respect, and honor.

To do well as a Mortuary Affairs Specialist, it is important to have good communication skills. You must be kind and patient. Mortuary Affairs Specialists must be able to be around sad things frequently.

> "They gave up all of their tomorrows so we could enjoy ours."
> —Unknown Navy Mortuary Affairs Specialist, Dover AFB

dignity (DIG-ni-tee): the quality or manner that makes a person worthy of honor or respect

Lights! Camera! Action! The military base talent show is one of the biggest events in a Recreation Specialist's year. They must use all of their skills to make the event run well and on time.

Recreation Service Specialists have many event-related responsibilities for events. They often work with **civilian** recreation staff to make plans. They must place advertisements in the base newspaper. They must select talent show judges and hire sound and lighting experts.

civilian (suh-VIL-yuhn): a person who is not a member of the armed forces or a police force

Recreation Specialists plan fun community activities for the base. No job is too big or small. For one event, they may serve cookies and punch at a reception. Another day, they might create the budget for the family fun day.

To do well as a Recreation Specialist, it is important to work well with others. You need to take care of many different tasks and be a leader.

ON BASE SERVICES

Most bases offer arts and crafts, bowling, community events, fitness, golf, outdoor recreation and more for military members and their families.

HAVING WHAT IT TAKES

Each Service Provider's job is different. At the heart of them all is the desire to serve others. Service Providers have the big job of promoting **esprit de corp** on military bases. It takes caring people to keep spirits high.

Do you like to help? Are you comfortable working with many different people? If so, you might be a good Service Provider.

ON THE JOB TRAINING

Service Providers attend basic military training and then get special training. However, many of the skills needed for a career in Services are learned on the job.

esprit de corp (ess-PREE duh kor): a feeling of pride and common loyalty within a group, community, or institution, such as branch of the military

MEMORY GAME

Look at the pictures. What do you remember reading on the pages where each image appeared?

INDEX

burial 20
competitions 8
cooking 12, 14
fitness 8, 10, 26
Guest Services 16

recreation 6, 24, 26
sports 8, 10
talent show 24
training 28

AFTER-READING QUESTIONS

1. Why is it important for Service Providers to like helping others?
2. What work schedule does a Service Provider have?
3. How many meals do Food Services Specialists prepare in one day worldwide?
4. What are intramural sports?
5. What are three kinds of work that Services Providers do?

ACTIVITY

Contact your City Parks and Recreation Department to find a Community Center near you. Ask your parents to take you there. Look to see what activities offered in your community are like military ones. Ask what it takes to attend.

ABOUT THE AUTHOR

J. P. is a veteran of the United States Air Force living in Metro Atlanta, Georgia. She now writes children's books that augment a child's classroom experience. J. P. is very excited to combine her love for writing with her military experience to produce the Careers in the US Military series.

© 2021 Rourke Educational Media

All rights reserved. No part of this book may be reproduced or utilized in any form or by any means, electronic or mechanical including photocopying, recording, or by any information storage and retrieval system without permission in writing from the publisher.

www.rourkeeducationalmedia.com

Quote sources: Connie Coats, interview with author.
USA Patriotism!, "Serving at the Air Force Mortuary Affairs Operations," YouTube Video, 3:55, September 16, 2014, https://www.youtube.com/watch?v=t972OXvFnpA.

PHOTO CREDITS: cover: ©Lance Cpl. Joseph Abrego/U.S. Marine Corps; page 4-5: ©mexrix/Shutterstock.com; page 5 (top): ©Cpl. Samantha K. Braun/U.S. Marine Corps/Department of Defense; page 5 (bottom): ©Lance Cpl. Dylon Grasso/U.S. Marine Corps; page 6-7: ©Mass Communication Specialist 1C Benjamin A. Lewis/U.S. Navy; page 8-9: ©fredrocko/Getty Images; page 9 (top): ©A1C Thomas Johns/DoD; page 9 (bottom): ©Steve Brown/U.S. Air Force; page 10-11: ©Tech. Sgt. Jeff Andrejcik/ U.S. Air Force; page 12-13: ©Mass Communication Specialist 2C Anthony N. Hilkowski/U.S. Navy/DoD; page 14-15: ©Fattyplace/Getty Images; page 15 (top): ©PH3 Lamel J. Hinton/U.S. Navy; page 15 (bottom): ©A1C Danny Monahan/U.S. Air Force; page 16-17: ©Stocktrek Images/Getty Images; page 18-19: ©Sergio Delle Vedove/Shutterstock.com; page 18: ©AlexLMX/Shutterstock.com; page 19 (top): ©DoD/Senior Airman Courtney Richardson; page 19 (bottom): ©U.S. Air Force A1C Keenan Berry/Released; page 20-21: ©Roman Valiev; page 21 (top): ©Staff Sgt. Bennie J. Davis III/U.S. Air Force; page 21 (bottom): ©Lance Cpl. Khoa Pelczar/DoD; page 22-23: ©narvikk/Getty Images; page 24-25: ©A1C Seraiah Hines/U.S. Air Force; page 26-27: ©Glynnis Jones/Shutterstock.com; page 28-29: ©U.S. Navy/ZUMA Press/Newscom

Edited by: Tracie Santos
Cover and interior design by: Alison Tracey

Library of Congress PCN Data

Service Providers / J. P. Miller
 (Careers in the US Military)
  ISBN 978-1-73164-357-5 (hard cover)(alk. paper)
  ISBN 978-1-73164-321-6 (soft cover)
  ISBN 978-1-73164-389-6 (e-Book)
  ISBN 978-1-73164-421-3 (ePub)
Library of Congress Control Number: 2020945586

Rourke Educational Media
Printed in the United States of America
01-3502011937